I Hear It the Way I Want It to Be

Poems by

David P. Kozinski

© 2022 David P. Kozinski. All rights reserved.
This material may not be reproduced in any form, published,
reprinted, recorded, performed, broadcast,
rewritten or redistributed without
the explicit permission of David P. Kozinski.
All such actions are strictly prohibited by law.

Cover art: "Snow from the Roof"
by Patricia Allis Mengers (photography)
Cover design by Shay Culligan

ISBN: 978-1-63980-062-9

Kelsay Books
502 South 1040 East, A-119
American Fork, Utah 84003
Kelsaybooks.com

For Walt Banker, Christopher Byrne, Francena Chalfant,
Sandra Ladley, Rick Marvin, David Rittenhouse
and Suzanne LeRoy Tea; lifelong friends

and always, Patti Allis, my best friend and so much more

Acknowledgments

Thanks to the publications in which some of these poems first appeared.

Anti-Heroin Chic: "My Theory of Relativity"

The Broadkill Review: "I Hear It the Way I Want It to Be," "Our Flimflam Affair," "Black Cat Bone," "Soirée dans Grenade," "After Wandering in the Morning," "Earthly Places"

Dreamstreets: "October Arrives in Sycamore Gold & Oak Bark Black," "What to Do with Anything"

Mad Swirl: "I Think That's Where I Put Them," "Old Love Song"

Moonstone Ink Anthology: "The other side of the pillow"

North of Oxford: "Find and Seek," "As Promised, the Fire"

One Art: "Arrivals/Departures," "Heavy, Heavy Metal"

Philadelphia Poets: "On the Heat and Recklessness of Late July"

Rabid Oak: "Regression"

Schuylkill Valley Journal: "Baldwin 1974," "The Seventies Came and Went," "Three or More Things to Keep in Mind"

Contents

I.

And then	9
Little Hunters	11
I Hear It the Way I Want It to Be	12
Baldwin 1974	14
The Seventies Came & Went	16
The other side of the pillow	17
The Cool Side and the Dark Face	18
The Trick	20
I Think That's Where I Put Them	22
Our Flimflam Affair	24
Black Cat Bone	26
Soirée dans Grenade	28
Find and Seek	29
All the Way Home	31
October Arrives in Sycamore Gold & Oak Bark Black	32
Night Watch	34
Late December Wedding	35
After Wandering In The Morning	36

II

Now you will be ashes, our conversation starts	39

III

Tear Them off One at a Time	49
As Promised, the Fire	50
At the Radiology Place	53
Arrivals/Departures	55
Old Love Song	56

Is it so much to ask	57
Three or More Things to Keep in Mind	59
On the Heat and Listlessness of Late July	61
What to Do with Anything	63
Earthly Places	65
My Theory of Relativity	66
November	67
Regression	68
I Would Sleep Through Busy Days	69
Heavy, Heavy Metal	71
Standing Still	72
The Old Spine	74
Wellspring	76
Planet of the Uncluttered Mind	79

I.

"Ever tried. Ever failed. No matter.
Try again. Fail again. Fail better."
—Samuel Beckett

And then

I became a family of one
in the first hour of December, the last car
of a train jogging heavily to the terminal.

I painted portraits of everyone I knew
as produce—the jolly king orange
and lithe banana, my friends the smug eggplant
and anxious pumpkin; gifted blueberries,
clever raspberries and cherries
        that tainted their lovers' fingers
     on the way into the agora
with nostalgia for tastes
their tongues never knew.
The figs and their wasp companions,
asparagus and I
vegged out to the voices of that late hour.

And then I sat on my sandy beach
and grieved the sunset like Alexander
bereft, nothing left to conquer—grandiosity
my only distraction—before flipping
           the calendar over
    like a game show host
without contestants.

Again I see a leaf caught in an eddy
like the one I saw
in the lone patch of youth's sunlight
the forest begrudged
        and the leaf's unselfconscious dance
    spurs the photographer
to arrest this moment and pin it
to a table of scrolls and cabrioles,
one that survived centuries of scribbling,

of cataclysm, even the humping, get-along gait
of the caterpillar
across its grain, perhaps

cousin to the one I find now, pausing
a moment to pose, then arching
across the right angle of sideline and service line,
      calibrating neither the court nor my concerns
on its way to another becoming.

The very next newspaper will read, *If you liked that
you're going to love this…*

Little Hunters

Chris painted Walenda
in tempura toppling
from the wire
    which must have been his worry.
Mine was the conductor
in a summer tux
    bringing down the world and its trappings
with the baton.

We all had these dreams of falling
or being let go,
of the insects
we killed and pinned
as a rite of passage to middle school,
    the red F
and *Come see me*
on the paper.

I'm still a slow reader and comprehension
is capricious
as a count in a comic opera.

There were scratchy wool suits in winter
      and a loneliness
that wouldn't dissolve.

I lost my place at the last recital,
too slow for the score
    so I stayed away from the piano
a while until it called me back
and since love
    was hard to find
I banged away at it
as long as I could.

I Hear It the Way I Want It to Be

Back in sixth grade,
as we smoked in Rockford Park
Chris joked about the blacking factory
where Dickens worked as a child.
I thought he meant the black king factory
where day after bleak nineteenth century day
boys our age toiled to produce one weak
but essential chess piece after another,
their grimy fingernails worn down,
pale faces set grimly, determined
to make each cut perfectly
and faster than the last time.

It seemed a natural: empire
accrued through the digits
of underfed tykes
carving pawns and castles and pointy-hatted
clergymen from nuggets of ebony
while over at the white king factory
their counterparts worked elephants' tusks.
All for export
all over the earth.
It was hard and cruel, but at least
they were making something
someone would use for fun.

I knew I should feel grateful
we spent our days learning fractions
and how the map of Europe changed so often.
I knew we were coddled and soft
and not like those boys who lost
parts of their fingers to machines
as my granddad had, some long time ago.

But from somewhere far above
and not too far in the future
I felt the squeeze coming—
to manufacture a more amusing game,
a better strategy for knocking down kings.

Baldwin 1974

With my brother studying abroad
the bigger-than-baby,
smaller-than-concert grand
that dominated my parents' living room
like a tuned-up, polished vehicle
was mine to bang on,
to experiment with; the lid raised,
the cage of metal cords
plucked with tongs or tapped
with a socket wrench.

I laid paper of varying hefts
across the strings of the top octaves
for percussion, a wooden ruler
across the bottom, hung
the old Sony reel-to-reel's microphone
like a trouble light under the hood.

We made tapes of everything
in our teens; the bathtub running, dog
barking, vacuum cleaner
and 'cello duets, the mantel clock chiming
Westminster, Wittenberg and *Winchester*
      running things faster and slower, backwards
and mashed all together. This was the field
he'd play on, the one my father put us out in early;
the one my family approved,
where Stefan thrived and I fooled around.

I played a little baseball
and loved football—relishing concussion
in helmet and pads,
scaring Mother, I knew, without her saying so

but seated in the cockpit
of the Baldwin or the Steinway at school,
power under my hands,
the smooth, flat white keys
and the candy bar black ones
at my fingers' choosing
I could drive the girls crazy
I thought.

Suzanne did sit still
now and then in the auditorium,
her loafers kicked off, rocking a leg
crossed over a knee
as my fingers mounted the steps of a scale,
urging her along with my left hand.

The Seventies Came & Went

All the train trips between Wilmington
and Philadelphia, New York,
Worcester and New London
were gray and solo;
frayed upholstery, a cocktail, a magazine
from the newsstand that flaked
green paint and smelled
of newsprint and cigars.

At Pennsylvania Station
while the train was resupplied, a punching bag
of a man lumbered through idle cars
selling papers. "T'dace noose,"
he intoned all the way down the aisle
and I overheard a couple of girls
in sweaters talking
about getting high between cars,
above the coupling,
once we were moving again.

It was a long way to Connecticut
when I was that young.
We lurched forward and were rolling
and I'd be half in the bag
when we piled out,
separated and met our rides.

It was always too cold,
(or too hot if I'd gone to D.C.)
and I waited for a ticket that exploded in my hand
but always woke with all my fingers
in a fist; thirsty, horny,
and excited to be somewhere else.

The other side of the pillow

was the other side of the moon
—unmapped, unexamined—place of promises
and answers, face known to Braille readers
and insomniac children,
articulated by sure fingers
and unacknowledged fears.

The other side of the pillow
was the sole refreshment in a nighttime
of desert walks and circular reasoning.

The flip side was sometimes better
than the "A" side, the coveted, unknowable face
worn but never seen.

        o   o   o

Now we know everything
about the undersides of ponds and planets,
hoard recipes in dream dishes
that can melt peoples away.

On the cool side of the pillow
we learn how the levers are wielded
and resisting bones broken.

Now we know the insides of bodies:
their systems and caches allow
for only so much tilt;
one life overturned
under a spotlight,
another under false flags.

The Cool Side and the Dark Face

No one can compartmentalize as well
as I think I can or see the seams
of the ball as it comes rushing up or hide
in many pigeon holes in multiple bureaus
so many things quickly classified.

The EKG suckers attach to my chest
and ankles the way a Cubist octopus
would try to grasp something too big
while the girl I spied in the anteroom
fiddling with her device waits sullenly
for test results, for liberating posts
that never come or come too late
or too early to appreciate.

There is nothing like the light show
of the EEGs I was given in grade school,
inaugurating an appetite like olives for gin
or ambergris for travel. The tests
were a production—the never explained
urine sample, staying up all night
so I'd nod off while the needles scratched
evidence of my unraveling.

Tonight the cool side of the pillow
like the dark face of the moon
opens a crack in a portal.
Cold when I lay down I woke overheated
in a nameless jurisdiction and now
the way back leads through the last sparks
disappearing into a pool.

Don't bother getting on
if you can't be attracted and revolted
in the same moment. This amusement
doesn't sound out syllables
in simple retrograde

and the hope of a long, good day rests
in a pill box locked away
in another box kept in a drawer
in a cabinet in a room
in one of many houses.

The Trick

You remember the bar in the Roosevelt Hotel,
the best part of an afternoon of crowds and chill,
spirits the color of the woodwork
around the room, fragrant evergreen swags.
I'd have stayed all night.

You remember hearing
the opening bars of "Hannibal"
for the first time; its muscular ostinato,
the peregrinations of the trumpet,
alto and keyboard along on a lark.

A rumble of thunder and you remember
the tides of love and safety flowed around you
like salt water, then washed
back into a turbulent, rolling force

and the drafty house
on that block of sweetly mismatched
fraternal twins; car alarms around the corners,
empty vials the size of perfume
samples on the sidewalk.

Don't forget Lufthansa, the grind
and bump of retracting wheels, the groans
of liftoff taking us out of 1984
and into another relentless winter.

You were sixteen when your father died.
I'll never forget
how tough you tried to appear
in your denim jacket and scuffed up boots.

You remember me, better or worse;
bourbon, musty books and blow,
the cats we adopted and the ones we buried
when their bodies failed; time run out.

How sick the world was: Cambodia, El Salvador,
Love Canal, Three Mile Island. How much it takes
to trick it back to health.

I Think That's Where I Put Them

If I were not still landlocked, in a state
between states
I would be forgiven all my lying-in
so long ago.
That was a few years into a prescription.
I learned to nap in an armchair,
narrow, upholstered,
under the Herald-Tribune.

To my left, a step up to a French door
and outside a balcony.
Below, a shaded garden, walled
the way they all were in that old tourist town.
My best stories follow the white pebbles
past snails that dream of the Duchy of Escargots
and on to the pavilion, its ping pong table
and rickety spinet with a few keys like nail-less fingers.

      o   o   o

Time liquefies, stretches like light.
What's left are forgetting and travel
and always peaks and glens
cut into a world that can be water, gas or ice.
Unlocked, a channel reveals
an island monastery
where I looked back from a great height.
Like everybody, I write what I remember;

the blue heat of adolescence
rising fast from the west and up my limbs,
sopping shoes pushing up worn stone stairs
as the rain slid down them like a fountain,

dining in the fading light on Brittany lamb, tasting
of the sea salt that washed the fodder
those babies ate, and below
the current gray and forever in flux.

Our Flimflam Affair

All the tumblers want to tilt when you're young
and waiting is long as it will ever be.
I met her accidently; smoking the kind
you can't get any more, in charge
of taking the money
to the window. It's easy to find somebody
who wants to help.
Wear a paint-streaked shirt
and good shoes and it won't take
an exceptional ear or a dog's nose
to sniff this one out. Establish position
in the middle of the room and wait.

Brilliant days she had a thick jacket
mostly tic or treat, mostly the kind of soft deals
that left them their dignity
if that's how they thought of it.

She couldn't draw a lick
or a strait that wasn't crooked.
She learned to see in the dark and drive
with no hands, recite lines from old movies
as if she made them up. I just did by speaking them.
The sound of laughter would ring
from a long neck knocked back, pearls palpating
smoother skin, reedy fingers combing
through a halo of ringlets.

Laws were memorized, the cases
that stacked up to them.
We could have practiced in any city
with a port, a park, chimneys
spelling out smutty jokes.

There were collections in a safe
deposit box I never saw, only the key
that caught light where it could.
There were ships on their way with skilled people
in containers bigger than my office.

I'd tell her what she'd get in her stocking,
in the kind of paper
that says an artist took this so hang onto it.
It'll be worth a pot some day.

Black Cat Bone

"'Cause I'm a voodoo child."
—Jimi Hendrix

Big houses turn me on.
Under the table
in her denim skirt
   and dark tights
she owns a cat's slow,
silent moves
   and lips
that set my whistle
for a long ride
     on a whipsaw road.
In the great room
at The Breakers we take
stately breakfasts,
   lots of slippery surfaces
      and rubber-meets-the-road
at a canter. Sunlight strains through doors
that open on pulsing masts
   and stunted grass, the sighing sails
that wring most of the Hoodoo
from my hands
   and leave the bitter bone.

We had trust and a future
   that opened like a hatbox
      and sounded like a bass drum,
took our time at New Year's brunch
at the brightest hotel in Spokane.
Half the people
     in Tabbi's hometown,
   so far from anywhere else,
knew I was turning 35
before I heard their names.

    Her hair grew back
wild from the chemo, the color
of bourbon and smoke.
    Her arms, silky
in their ebony opera gloves,
        held and pulled me like a tide
    before her nails opened gashes
that stranded us on an unfamiliar shore.

Soirée dans Grenade

    after Claude Debussy

Mix a quip with a droplet of Cinzano
and an olive in an ice cube
and lean forward to suggest attention.

It is, after all, transactional.

Look at her magenta lips as they pronounce *argent*
and make eye contact but don't bore in.
You're not taking a biopsy.

She's taking requests.

A little Spanish fly may flutter up
from under the bridge of her guitar
and buzz around the rafters.

This and the heat could prove distracting.
The ice and everything melts quickly in these climes
marking the time you have.

Her irises turn lavender

which is my favorite scent. Yours too?
You may have more time than I thought.
Count the hibiscus blossoms silently

in the honeydrip of twilight

and concentrate on her tune,
languid and undulating between modes
that won't be pinned down.

They only live in these strings.

Find and Seek

I call you but you are out in the yard
where dragonflies flit and mate in midair
and ants patrol the peonies,
where you overturn shovels full of earth,
bury bitterness in a scarf
like one you draped over the violin
when you tucked it in its case.

I call for you and from your sickbed
a response quieter than the hum
of streetlamps. A puzzle, an answer
arrive in headlights curling
around a shadowed bend in our road.

I call out for you
and you are there for me
until you are not.

There are more rooms in our house than I knew.
Each door opens to another room,
another door; cupboards of implements,
summer garments from another time
hanging in a closet with a window,
drawers with files of records
and little mysteries—a whistle, cufflinks and studs,
a long letter that urges reason and rhyme.

"One place for this, another for something else,"
I think aloud, moving through them
all in dimming light.

I called to you at dusk and again this morning
and you were next to me, the fragrance
of your chest, the smooth
skin of your limbs.

I called out a warning, a prophecy
and it was a claim cordoned off
and conveyed, an alias
of ill-fitting clothes.

All the Way Home

The airliner, crammed full, hums
above covering clouds—comforters
of a sickly world. But you can't sleep

through everything. We're in trouble.
Tweeting senators twit and twat.
This marks a hitch in development
or a decadence of empire,

rhythms not just broken but forgotten:
mammoths gathering wool
not long ago beside the Great Lakes
which were called something else or nothing yet,

then sweat and harvest, rising and falling back
to dust, retreat to winter.
Mayday Mayday intone the pilots
as engines fly apart and behold, below

the levees crumble. *Moloch Moloch
Moloch Moloch* said the crazy poet in a bathrobe
who flew through the Rockies,
harmonium stowed overhead

and some who heard him chanting
recognized the name, clucked
and tucked their heads
neatly under their wings.

October Arrives in Sycamore Gold & Oak Bark Black

A long summer ends with forsythia
tinted rose, then plum; a dying pear tree
and freight trains knocking
the window panes. The tracks etch
an incision scar along the river
and some nights the wind
pulls the essence of garbage dump
and holds it over this part of town.
It chokes like a queen of clubs
that drops on the last trick you needed.

My long summer ends with mourning
a young poet and a dislocated shoulder.
The august Dr. Nutsenbolts shuffles in,
glances at it, says
you have two choices and describes the surgery.
"What's the other choice?"
*Don't operate and your arm becomes a decorative thing
hanging from your shoulder.*

A year ends with much to look toward

    though this may seem like looking in a mirror
    that faces a mirror

and to look back on in lights
that pierce night's dome—

    clove and bay leaf in the kindergarten,
    vanilla extract dribbled into warm milk
when I couldn't sleep

    numbing water sliding over stones
to the river that would not be dammed
even long enough to remember the loved and gone,
    a voice that speaks
only from the page
of landing at inhospitable ports
and about fire escapes and steep embankments.

It ends as I lift my arm to wave
to the woman who can laugh with me
when there isn't much to laugh about.

Night Watch

Tonight was so quiet
I saw three cars, no pedestrians
and seven deer—eyes and ears aimed
my way, not an antler among them.
They didn't run, ambled up a slope
as I approached within thirty yards.
What I know about hunting fits in this sentence.
*What's the challenge in dropping
one of these with a rifle. Are they tame?*
Under the bridge, the crescent
undulates in a backwater
and someone a league distant
sees its double in another little creek
while our cousin, far away,
ventures a dry prayer.

Walking back, a few houses are lit
with computer screens,
a television's blue gaze,
while others lie dark as closed eyes.
A walk to the mailbox would find me
across from the site of a couple of killings
and several deals gone bad, the orange taint
of neon on the clouds. I mean hot-blooded
murders that triangulated love, aspiration
and despair inside three story boxes
with balconies for jaws and ungenerous walls.
Last winter someone camped
in a lean-to of trash and twigs in the woods
and it wasn't for fun. This land
was too cold for that.

Late December Wedding

The girls dance together
crackling in the warmth
and pounding bass.

Between the carriage house and the mansion
proper, a few little ridges of snow are lit
with cold, gold LEDs, dying their long death.

This park with its ghost ship run aground,
its rocks and gullies, would have been a great place
for kids to get high and steam up their windows.

A county car sleeps under the festooned trees.
The reception adjourns. There are too many
pricey houses nearby to allow much fun.

If there are hungry people around here
they won't be seen
and those without homes don't make it this far.

Stop thinking about what is lost
and end up unable to stop thinking
about what there is to lose, because

all around the country chests are thumped
and loneliness sojourns
in town after town that doesn't know what it wants.

After Wandering In The Morning

"Da kam ich auf einen breiten Weg."
—from "Urlicht"

I came upon a broad path
and yes, an angel with an owl's umber wings
upheld a blade orange as sunset
to turn me away.

Nearby the riddling water foamed with life.

I started him talking and he lowered his sword.
At noon we laughed together
until I forgot why
I turned to cross the bridge.

I'd meant to convince him
I was returning home, nothing
more, but turning found myself
in different clothes, tripping

back down the way I'd come
aware an opening
to something long desired
had closed finally.

Though earth quieted I remained restless.

Along the road green leaves that greeted
the morning blistered in the slanting sun
and every familiar root and stone
lay blanketed in crimson.

II

"And the noise is as much as I can bear."
—PJ Harvey

Now you will be ashes, our conversation starts

In Memoriam—Stefan Brock Kozinski

"Nutrisco et extinguo."—Motto of Francois I of France

"Do not take up music unless you would rather die than not do so."
—Nadia Boulanger

Instead of early morning
across time zones for our one-sided talk
—your dime, your time—
we travel, back in time at first,
to watch the building of those horseshoe stairs,
then to descend
    three hundred years forward
        to the front yard of the *adieu*
            the place where you thrived
        and words first trickled
            in from my naps after breakfast,
    pooled gradually at first,
then shot up like fountains.
    Dry Julys, the cool days of August
there really was hunting to be done
in the hodge-podge of architecture,
crush of tour buses, regiments of flowers,
champagne buzz and falling grandeur
of the old king's lodge, his salamanders
basking in relief on the walls.
    That was the palace of our growing up.
Yeah, there were preludes—school bullies
and neuroses, choir robes and distant relatives
—but these lines, brother, speak of flights and fires.

At the mouth of the staircase—two-pronged fork—
a twenty-something pianist hurried past
in a t-shirt that read *Fugue You*.

It was the summer of the moon landing
and Nixon ascending, the flipped bird
of his nose everywhere.

Back home, around a corner table
at the Wild Goose Inn
pass a bottle of cheap scotch,
      tilt at the mills
that stamp out musical soma,
      at the factories for wax soldiers
and holy wars. Later we take up
the 'cello and fiddle, slip crickets
through the scrolls,
invite owls to roost in pianos,
drive around all night; headlights off
and 8-cylinder Bartok on the radio;
Sun Ra tripping in the glove box,
his band clanging and droning
like New Year's mummers.
      Instead of tossing a football
we ran the tapes backwards and sideways,
at Thanksgiving; sped them up, mixed
a toxic radio preacher's "God acted alone," ("duh"),
a sawed-off viola and trash can percussion
with the bard owl's lunatic comments
lifted from a 78 RPM record of bird songs.

I repeatedly unscrewed the jar-o, gulped
and damped my hammer and anvil,
clouded synapses and synesthetic spume.

You drafted your tonal papers
on a chalky board—bold letters
to gurus and government czars,

dazzling maestros
and tanned debutantes.
    When they answered we jammed
them all in the back seat—fill 'er up—and made
for the old headmaster's lawn,
leaving donuts just hours
before tee-time.

Maybe we didn't do all that,
just boxed odious ideas to a standoff,
tried to forget our dear, bloody country's
gunned down heroes and Vietnam meat grinder:
keeping busy and staying tight, respectively.

        o   o   o

Now I carry the four pages
to the lectern and revisit passages
from our long ago when I followed you
like a fan—trains to Princeton Junction,
to Gare de Lyon, Chelsea; airplanes to Spokane,
Hannover, Dessau. The church is still adorned
like rich people's Christmas
where you presided at the organ,
where mothers' voices
    rang out from under veiled hats
        remember those? I can see
the girl in pale lip gloss, nipples probing
unexplored space. She sang
with her new-hatched chest thrust out
for me and the boys, we thought.
I should know better now. She sang
of her thirteen springs,

of her body's modest blooming
and the god-is-love safety surrounding us.

I start to read a eulogy, written in one night.
You've gone so fast there wasn't time
to compose. I don't begin, *Once upon a time*
but I admitted the typing fairy
      that cobbled me a pair
    of uneven legs while I slept.
I'd do it differently now,
like fucking almost everything.
Unlike all the haphazard choices,
the friends who've stayed turned out well.
      Every kneeling pad is needle-pointed
with an icon—a fish, three crowns, a cross,
and we stand up and sit down a few times
mouthing old words, familiar rhythms.
    They pack us in pews as young sardines,
these institutions: tabulae rasae, thirsty minds
accept faulty explanations that drip, drip
drip until they must be true.

        o   o   o

Overnight we changed the number of the year:
something broken arriving from overseas
      in a polished, ebony box.

Alarms sound, muffled
and distant. It pains me
to feel so little. Brother, walk down
with me through the cool shadows

and fragrant lanes—boxwood lined corridors
      that squeezed ideas into light
   that brought your pianist's fingers,
pen and ruler, to paper.

This theft will always trouble me, won't it?
   More elegantly executed
than a suicide squeeze; scribed
and studied by investment bankers
and Ponzi wizards, the artists of our era
   who paint new heavens
on our ceilings—faux gold leaf,
superhero cartoons.

I have unfinished business but am still
unsure what business we were in:
songs, box scores, human accounts
and sublimely shipwrecked hearts.

What you noted, scored
into lined pages, what's left of you
on creaky reels and shiny discs
lodge in my vault
guarded by multi-headed dragons
retrofitted with guided missiles and cop killa caps.

   You'd say,
Friends, let's strike more joyful noises.
Don't even offer the ram to these arrivistes,
these wee, bloodthirsty gods.
Say that I've left tickets for them
at Will-call. Give the dog in the manger
an extra biscuit and a scratch behind the ears.

Death is a short sleep, you repeat
taking it from the top,
knowing I'll never believe it.
I'll listen for your voices, many instruments,
and hear them when I'm climbing, wheezing along.

       o   o   o

One night we consoled Dad,
the first and only time, his reservoir
of confidence running to the edges
of the table and down
to a floor of Rorschach shapes.
    I'd felt the anxious power
of amphetamine rising
through my heart to my brain
and out of my hands
until the whiskey did its work.

We were all shaken
and I stumbled out into the clatter
of cicadas and katydids, seeking
a particular solitude
that slipped farther away
with each step.
    In childhood the only reassuring tales
were ticks and whispers of our house
        same age as you
settling like an old man's spine
as I grew unsteadily;
the tapping typing of the mechanic's son
at the kitchen table, a kitten climbing
his pants leg with baby claws;

mother with her soft pencils
and easy eraser hustling in with a basket
of wind-blown laundry,
singing, "diamonds are a girl's best friend,"
in her still-young voice,
"and every twenty years another war;"
      you at the piano
diving into the engulfed cathedral.

Then, there were your variations
and then our verses.

There had to have been two of us
because I say every day a curse
and you would never have it so.
    There'll be no procession, no hearse
and instead of knowing where to go
I'll drive in loops around the reservoir,
past the place where the Impala
rolled right through steel cords, spun 180°
and settled on the soft shoulder
where I woke; where you, the elder,
      would have found me
   and taken me home.

III

"For the sky and the sea, and the sea and the sky
Lay dead like a load on my weary eye"
—Samuel Taylor Coleridge,
"The Rime of the Ancient Mariner"

Tear Them off One at a Time

It still isn't clear what was to come next.
There was a plot but even dreams changed
    sweat-damp pajamas and a bank of red telephones
rang as often as I slept.

There were no easy days
even if someone steered
    the cigar wasn't going to smoke itself
or the lamps keep themselves trimmed and burning.

They scraped one brother's lung, right here
at home, took another's leg. Mr. Best of Bremen
offered tolling bells as he handed off the urn
to bring the other brother home with the suitcases.

I can't move my hands
enough to rake a campus for ideas that sound
original, to cover futility with earth.
The days are torn away.

As Promised, the Fire

In the heat I saw colors
no one else could or cared about.

In the fire we lost most
of the things I cared about.
The wills, birth certificates, passports
were lodged at the bank. The art
became smoke,
then a charcoal smudge.

In the fire I smelled apple and azalea,
cedar and hemlock,
mother and father;
what they worked for.

Far from any city
stars burned holes in the skin
of my dream time. Laughter, sirens
spun rings around the world.

I was offered in the fire
the hope of revolution and stasis.

I lost people I loved during the years
of occupation. Not dead, they were misplaced,
stuck away in cupboards, hidden
in lockers, in paperwork. I sought
and could not find them again.

I heard much in the darkness
you brought with you. Most
of the captured images came clear.

You lost people too.
You prayed for them.
They died, their lights went out
and others could be seen.
Everything burned, even things
you wouldn't expect: rivers and harbors,
identities, principles many
boasted they'd die for.

I saw the colors of ideas, some
for just a moment, while others burned
into my palette. The more profound,
the duller the hues—matte-finished gun metal,
hospital green—while funny little concepts
rose like globes from a soap bubble pipe
and popped right out of existence.

From where we huddled
dying stars sounded
like the shrieks of toads when they jump
from embankment to water, gone in the ripples.

Even the thick doors of perception
shut bank-vault tight, tall
as cathedral spires, went up.
At the end, geysers erected
steam towers to sustain the sky,
to hold it back.

Some authorities told me about cold fire
that cuts through the hardest hearts,
arteries pulsing with angry lorries
and crazy cabs. I reminded them

the avenues and boulevards are also strolled
by hand-in-hand youth,
by skeptics as well as cynics.

There's no shame in sweat, I told them,
even the kind that poisons
the very ground when flicked
over a garden wall.

I asked these magi for references
that might unlock my box of promises
where the bedeviling of man
is kept down, churning in mushroom dark.

I read to them as they lay in blindness,
fallen into adult beds with linen
as dirty as any hospital could make it,
infirmity our timekeeper.

At the Radiology Place

Fail better, Beckett exhorts
and that is too much to ask
days when there is no consolation
to offer the girl who sees in the broken
medicine cabinet door a metaphor
for her daddy's stolen years.

Shite, her father, my brother Michael,
went down fighting,
his racquet waiting in the car
for the game he was certain he'd play
any day now.
    My brother Stefan
wasn't ready to go, either,
but there was no one by his bed
to laugh with, to toast or complain
about, to study in the infinity
mirror or bid goodnight. Just
the music playing in his head that morning
that arrived as usual too early–
Boulanger, perhaps, or Busoni.

I may be the one cursed
to hang around, haunting, long
past the hour of giving up.

Lying on my side for the x-rays
it occurs to me maybe
what they're not telling us
is, the more we inhale and sit still
for these pictures the more
we're immunized and death
postponed—a perverse conspiracy,

keeping the gospel from us.
        If the story got out
there'd be a stampede to every
hospital and testing clinic
and somebody would have to pay.

This notion makes it hard
to keep still. I stifle a chuckle
and dial up the saddest thought
there is—the kids who never learn
to fall, whose weeks and months roll by
and leave them afraid to fail at all.

Arrivals/Departures

The woman I don't recognize
except in the glitter and ruins of dreamland
looks a little like Diana Krall,
tells me her father died,
not when or how

and I wrap my rough hand over hers
the way paper overcomes rock,
the way overcoming can shield and heal
and say in the commonest way
I don't have words
for moments like this.

As if the two are related
she adds, "I was born at the airport."
Maybe she means came into the world
with baggage. Maybe she means
people only pause, in transit.

I summon a look of understanding
to my eyes and lay my hand
flat on the table
parallel to hers, so that together
they shape something wingèd
at rest, contemplating flight.

Old Love Song

I've never told a whole story
in one arm-length sheet
the way some can.
In hours drawn across glass
the floorboards are the loose lips
that expose my coming and going.

If my hand stayed in
it was for the sake of another
who opened her eyes
one night the firmament rang
& the shrapnel of stars, full-throated,
sang out in all the languages.

With her there were no acid tears,
only anger turned inward
then out—a lightning tongue—and relish
of the world's buffooneries.
Every tale was a sleeve
that could be lengthened or shortened

right on the dressmaker's dummy,
cuffs added, buttons sewn or severed.
They were not always the ones
I wanted to hear
but sounded dense and deep
as Russian bells.

Is it so much to ask

having a sandwich named after me

or a building, a tall, gleaming tower
or a bridge with a noble brow
and a half-dozen suicides?

Back to the sandwich. It could be introduced
to the public by a turtle wearing a top hat
and tails, and a cat with a clarinet
and licorice tail.

You know how I am
        fanciful but simple
in my tastes
yearning for what is original,
reaching for the grand.

If all the sandwiches and buildings and bridges
are taken, it could be a forest preserve.
Mountains rise, shadowed and misty
and the surrounding trees
stand thickly and territorial briars prickly.
Can you picture it?

But I'd rather have the sandwich—something
good with soup—seedless rye with a thin layer
of mixed mayonnaise and Dijon mustard, spread
all the way out to the crust, or maybe with pesto
but definitely with bacon and turkey

so that I'll have a reason
        and not an excuse

when I drift off
after our long conversation.
Alas, no sandwich, no monument
can compensate for everything
I leave undone—peace treaties and climate accords,
clothing the naked, housing the dispossessed;
the return of traditional American values—60 cent a gallon
gasoline and cigarettes @ 50 cents a pack;

no sandwich
can let the legless walk or the fearful run again,
reverse the course of rivers
or give the horseshoe crab time to evolve

and in this soured age
who is there to ask
to make it so?

Three or More Things to Keep in Mind

Don't let stomach distress
or digestive difficulty
interfere with your active life-
style. Used as directed, Oxipep© (Oxivipepsinol)
will quickly have you horseback riding,
mountain climbing, elatedly sharing
a stunning vista from twin bathtubs
with a youthful, attractive companion
or, if you're old, merrily tandem biking.

Take it two to three times a day
or maybe four to six times a day.
Oh hell, take it as much as you want!
It's doctor-recommended. And doctors
aren't allowed to do harm. Nothing will go wrong.
Stop worrying and get ready to do things
you've never tried before.
Hitching a ride on a slow-moving
freight train is fun. So is drag racing
on the Autobahn.
Explore the White House grounds.
The fence isn't that high.

> May cause upset stomach, drowsiness, dizziness or giddiness. May lead to shortness of breath, sinusitis, rash, acid reflux, a nagging sense of disappointment and disgust, nausea and vomiting. May cause wakeful dreaming, visions of rocks melting and time freezing, visions of burning seas and laughing trees, blurred vision, double vision or lack of vision. May intensify feelings of depression or elation. Reverse menopause has occurred. In rare cases users

have experienced arrhythmia, internal bleeding,
convulsions and death.

Do not stop using Oxipep
abruptly or without consulting
your doctor, who, as you recall
will do no harm. While using this medication
inform your doctor of any planned
surgical or dental procedures,
of vaccinations required for foreign
travel, of the sort of traveling
you'll be doing and how long
you'll be overseas. Business
or pleasure?

Will you have a house-sitter
or will your place be empty and quiet,
off the road as it is?
Are you running away
from something?
Have you recently
experienced inexplicable feelings
of guilt?
Maybe you'd better not
leave town.

What were the three things I asked you
to remember?

On the Heat and Listlessness of Late July

In the back stretch of boys' summer
the windfall of free time
was spent down and routines lay in wait
like highwaymen who'd kill
the shotgun rider, cow the teamster,
and, at leisure, paw through women's trunks
with gloved hands,
pocket men's gold watches,
discarding their studs.

It's like being an only child without the advantages
I remember thinking, kicking smoothed stones
under the bridge like a grade school troll
as I inhaled the cocktail of fresh
and stagnant water and felt around
slimy stones between the minnows
for a dropped trinket.

Every summer was stolen from us
Phillies fans and reading list drudges
who holed up in cool rooms
and padded chairs, tried to stir up a thrill
with pointless shoplifting
and played pick-up games
in dusty fields on graying grass.
The mustard light at dusk found
skunk cabbage and poison ivy,
held off the impending loss of the freedom
that made days expendable and dear.

Now, in my 59th year
a ghostly Chico Ruiz steals home again,

finishing the picadors' work.
It was a bonehead play that started
the great collapse in '64.
Now the boneheads rule,
unfathomable pinheadery triumphs,
and much more is taken
than gold or dignity
or a season of hope.

What to Do with Anything

No matter who handled the wheel
it was all over the road—noisy gears
and the likelihood of ending
turned around on the bank
    off the shoulder. Sand accrued there
interestingly enough to wonder
and when the rubber
sank softly as gums
    the night swallowed
and we rolled out.

It was all over the road
and surrounding settlement
that the course was erratic or worse
un-soldierly and that nothing
in the way of wings peeked
up out of those soft shoulders
    nothing seeped from those cool eyes
and get-down mouth
while the scuttlebutt
buffeted against her striking heart.

I bought a cheap parlay
    took a flier on a tranche
of refrigerator boxes and submerged paper.
This is the only way to chew
a cherry here in Delaware
(everything else being sewn shut)
on a summer night, full-ish moon
with all that portent hanging in the trees
    the hashish tasting a little of sausage
and sage in the safety of the paddock.

Dice laughed on the table
like a chatter of death
and there were a few Darvon
in a drawer. In the morning bees
would be back but for now mostly crickets
did the talking. Eyes like jellied fire, Ruthie
and Sara Beth compared the colors
of their petals—coral, tan and putty—
willows sifting a breeze—and it didn't matter
what I did with my hands.

Earthly Places

"And all that I knew is moving away from me."
—Joanna Newsom

The sign on the office door reads
Gone where the clock really jumps from the wall
in exasperation at the lateness of hours,
where donkeys spit eulogies that fall
like bricklebrit in the palms of refugees.

Yes, it is a long message
because in places like that
gears reconsider why they are and retard
their turning; the key fits and the latch
slips open, spoons fill themselves
and moonless, drifting evenings fork.

In such a place
the song I wanted to remember
lingers in that first terrible moment
of waking and there is just a sputter
of time to profitably
retrace my trespasses.

My Theory of Relativity

> "I look at maps of Mirny Mine. / They blur and sink away in salt water…
> I have work in an hour / and a hole in the ground /
> large enough to be seen from space"
>
> —Elizabeth Leo

This is about the kindness
of a dog and how a human should be,
a little about cruelty,
but mostly about scale—how vast
it all appears; the indifference
of the bluest fields
and the nearest, newest moon.

Friends, when I say *this is about*
I mean history; the day and night, sleep
and travel, tenderness and the grinder.
In another hour the sands might still,
the glass stopper itself; hands
gesture to nothing

but nothing unstopped stays the same.
The silo empties as regularly
as a lab rat's feeder.
Whatever first lifts us up
from then on pulls down—the perpetual
drizzle, the unsolvable
argument of a trench seen from space
and the chasm so deep under water
where every story runs in its own time.

November

    for Bill Hetznecker

After the unforgiving day that stretched,
tore like a tendon, snapped off like a lamp

my friend's voice edges through darkness
and white noise—lantern in the fog—

not with the comfort he brought all his life
but to say what waits is not better or worse

but indescribably, dimensionally different,
unknowable with human equipment

and that fearing it or coveting it
might be the only real sins.

I want to say *Thank you, Bill—a father*
when I'd longed for and forgiven my own,

sharp-eyed brother-in-arms, sure-armed oarsman
but my words dissolve on my tongue

and the source of what it seemed I heard drifts away.
I skate, impossibly, down a promenade

canted like a luge chute, into the vale
where torchlight and shadow vie in the grizzled hills.

Regression

> "Climate is what you expect. Weather is what you get."
> —Mark Twain

The fan hums
it's too hot to read
and I nod and close the book.

The meat of my hand
sticks to paper, the pen
dries up and I close them
in a drawer.

Dead things and picked fruit
rot fast and old folks
who don't make it
to the movies or the mall die.

Would it break us to deliver
an air conditioner
to each stifling garret?
Drivers and lifters
grateful for the work,
might tip their caps, accept
a glass of cold water.

My grandmas didn't succumb
to heat. Lucky, they died old
and cared about
and not by their lonesomes.
Through war and armistice
and war the iceman stumped
through their homes.

I Would Sleep Through Busy Days

This book has been writing
itself. I mean it: my keypad taps away
while I snooze. The manuscript strides
handsomely and truly toward its ending
flexing panther's muscles.

A dry cough admonishes
we avoid *making overtures*
or *indulging in recapitulations*,
even with the supply of music
drying up like dying rivers.
The tapping continues anyway.
Nothing peripheral or centrifugal, please,
from that selfsame voice.
I say rulers are meant
to be snapped in half over a hard knee
or picked off by lone men
posted in cheering crowds.
      Tap tap tap.

I'm winded after a few stairs
but the book runs a half marathon and looks
ready to strip its cover off and take a long swim.
Will my volume end its days
bedridden and worm-eaten
I think aloud
in the pet products, cleaning supplies
and paper goods aisle of the smallest
supermarket in New Castle County.
Could a book watch too many
Aquaman cartoons for its own good?

Of course it could. It did.

It may not be taken
for long as a good book but for now
it is an apt pupil, the William Tell apple,
the Best New Show of a slow season.
It is the call of crows that land awkwardly
on a shaggy green lawn
on a sumptuous spring morning
when dogs bark the news back and forth
between the houses of neighbors
who haven't time for pleasure reading.

Heavy, Heavy Metal

You finally find your row
and your seat, looking forward
to a night that lifts and bounces,
that stickily edges you when it can
to its or anyone's full-body tease
unmasked, at ease. What remains is fog
hanging like crepe, unsupported;
willows billowing.

And just like that, the re-humpty-dumptification
of the egg industry and other slight miracles
are accomplished, and release comes
at the end of a chain of trumpets and trombones
which is to say it's brassy—sounds it, feels it
even tastes it. The saliva drips thinly
from the clarinet's bell
and the chimes and lyre
stir a roux of black Sabbath.

Standing Still

About the time I recognize it
love ebbs, leaving cleansed sand
and polished glass, a cast
of starfish and urchins.

Coping with loss flows one way
for mother, another for father; nowhere
with brother and sister.
There are some I should not, should not
have survived and many more
I will not—open-mouthed throng.

Suggestions become guidelines
and then thick rules of thumb harden
into laws. It's not that I expect
everything to stand still but I've thumbed
my nose sore at good advice
and jarred the rest like preserves.

Paralyzed when we dream
deeply, it's harder to fall
from high limbs should we find ourselves
chasing or chased, bending
to pick summer's berries
or pull bones from the fire.

That this inaction persists into waking
is not excused but explained.
Hobbled instinct, spurred decisions
cost me strength and peace
and what they can buy.

The children long to be listened to
and I would oblige them, standing
to receive and record what they cry out,
pronouncing the syllables back to them.
It is the deadliest game we are playing

and there is no catching them
near the cliffs or fetching
them from chasms, even if
they wish to be returned.
They are starving, big as they are.

The Old Spine

"Been a long time crossing Bridge of Sighs"
—Robin Trower

Days when I am able
to not think about the worst things that happen
in the world
—you know what they are—
I can forget about feeling

that bits and pieces are being amputated
or disabled—a much-valued thumb,
my tricuspid valve that steadies the stream
of blood and joy, that little cut of neocortex
that stops me taking myself too seriously.

I felt my grip loosening as I read
at my father's memorial and at mother's
I was shaky and gray as the cigarette butt
smoked to a roach and flicked
on that golf course-green churchyard.

Standing in the sunlight at the sculptor's graveside
a tooth chipped out
and at the party to celebrate the poet
the hors d'œuvres were like communion wafers
on my tongue—an unyielding paste.

Something furtive subtracts from my little piles
of coins, of uncorrupted moments,
the maze master mouse nibbling at the edge of sleep,
pinching the bait, bit by bit. No, something else
sieves the colors, dilutes the proof.

The damp field smell of fall goes first
and "Missing:" posters the size of Post-its pop up
everywhere I turn. Vanished are the pine needles
that stuck to her skirt like evidence, and gone
the sound of the engine taking us across

the bridge for giddy self-medication,
the groaning of the span,
an old spine
bearing the weight and business
of all that traffic.

Wellspring

    for P.A.M.

If I steal a horse for you
I will close the barn door with a hush after us.

If we share the horse and ride quickly
we'll see everything through the same eyes.

When we steal horses together
it's only for a joyride. When we're breathless
and saddle sore we dismount
and send them home.

You say, "If they catch us
there'll be a hanging," pointing your alien hat
to the horizon. "If they catch me they'll wish
they'd gone fishing offshore," I answer,
chin up, staring down my nose.
Chill and whisper go aloft.
"Strange and safe," you reply, "milk safe
and surgeon strange."

        o   o   o

If we ride far into another country
we'll need a translator to tune it up.

It is a place of overlapping arrondissements;
eccentric circles of Three-card Monte
and lobbying, irregular ovals
of night time streetwalkers
and morning street cleaners.

In the new country the music
is hard and overwhelming—undammed
water to draft and drown in.
As we're playing an elastic score
you'll attend the stricken
while I watch over you.

If they come to extradite us
I will tell them we have taken only
the idea of souls.

If everything of ours passes
the cutting room, we'll be stamped
and moved along.
When we return home
we own all the land and make the manners.

When everything is lashed
and ready, the mortgage loosens its grip,
the fee simpler than ever.

Say these words: easement, escheat,
adverse possession. Everything is still
and ready in the Spanish room.
Something waits for someone in there,
something I've left in a chest
with a deft, doctor's hand,
opened with a seldom spoken spell.

   o   o   o

It begins in the eye and races down
through meadow and fragrant dale alike,

across land and sea. Such is devotion
that reinforces and reinvents
with only an arrow to guide.

If we offend, let us take more than horses
or faulty explanations.

We will have what we will
and divvy among the deserving
a foundation.

We will hold the wellspring
our grace, and affection
to ourselves.

If it is love that locks the box, that starts
and ends a war, it also transcribes
all the raw you want to say.
Bring the last draft to me
at the end of my days.

Planet of the Uncluttered Mind

There is a distant place
where the one-word poem is highly valued.

It can describe a tangible thing
    a thought or emotion
or comprise a combination of what words do.

It can take the poet years
    sometimes a lifetime
while the word evolves.

I'm not going there.

About the Author

David P. Kozinski was a finalist for the Inlandia (California) Institute's 2020 Hillary Gravendyke Prize for the original manuscript of this book. He is the recipient of an Established Professional poetry fellowship from the Delaware Division of the Arts. His full-length book of poems, *Tripping Over Memorial Day* was published by Kelsay Books and he won the Dogfish Head Poetry Prize, which included publication of his chapbook, *Loopholes* (Broadkill Press). Expressive Path, a non-profit that facilitates youth participation in the arts, named him 2018 Mentor of the Year. For his poetry and visual art, Kozinski received the Dr. Eugene Szatkowski Award from the Americans of Polish Descent Cultural Society of Delaware. He was selected by Robert Bly to attend his workshop sponsored by the *American Poetry Review*. He serves on the editorial board of *Philadelphia Stories* and is Art Editor of *Schuylkill Valley Journal*. He is the resident poet at Rockwood Park & Museum in New Castle County, Delaware.

www.ingramcontent.com/pod-product-compliance
Lightning Source LLC
Chambersburg PA
CBHW021023090426
42738CB00007B/885